LEARN TO DRAW

DISNEY PRINCESS

Favorite Princesses

Featuring Tiana, Cinderella, Ariel,
Snow White, Belle, and other characters!

New edition now featuring Merida & Rapunzel!

Walter Foster Jr.

MIX
Paper from
responsible sources
FSC® C101537

Published by Walter Foster Jr., an imprint of The Quarto Group.
6 Orchard Road, Suite 100, Lake Forest, CA 92630
www.QuartoKnows.com

Printed in China
13 15 17 19 18 16 14

Table of Contents

Tools & Materials

You'll need only a few supplies to create all of your favorite Disney princesses. You may prefer working with a drawing pencil to begin with, and it's always a good idea to have a pencil sharpener and an eraser nearby. When you've finished drawing, you can add color with felt-tip markers, colored pencils, watercolors, or acrylic paint. The choice is yours!

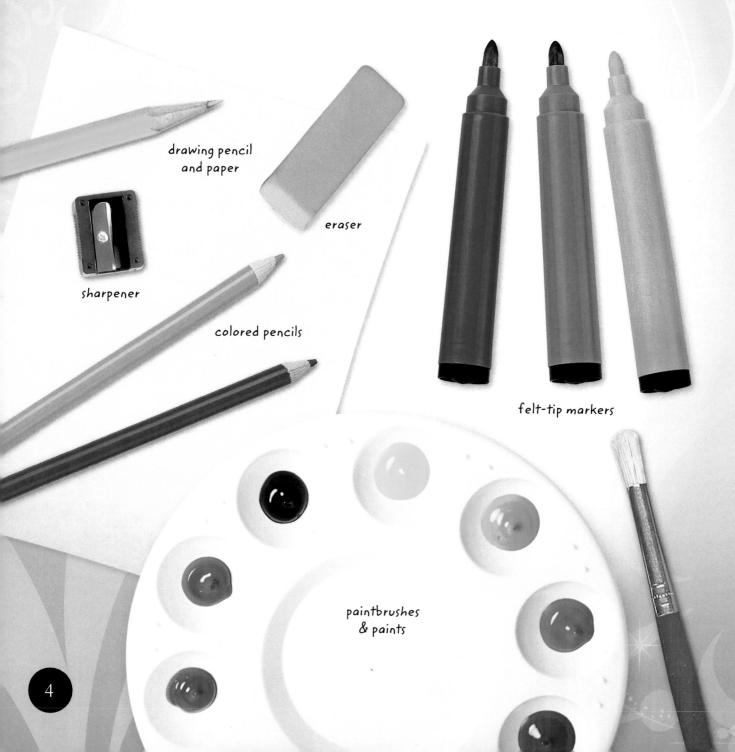

drawing pencil
and paper

eraser

sharpener

colored pencils

felt-tip markers

paintbrushes
& paints

How to Use This Book

In this book you'll learn to draw your favorite princesses—and a few of their friends—in just a few simple steps. You'll also get lots of helpful tips and useful information from Disney artists that will guide you through the drawing process. With a little practice, you'll soon be producing successful drawings of your own!

Step 1
First draw the basic shapes using light lines that will be easy to erase.

Step 2
Each new step is shown in blue, so you'll know what to draw next.

Step 3
Follow the blue lines to draw the details.

Step 4
Now darken the lines you want to keep, and erase the rest.

Step 5
Use some magic (or crayons or markers) to add color to your drawing!

Drawing Exercises

Warm up your hand by drawing squiggles and shapes on a piece of scrap paper.

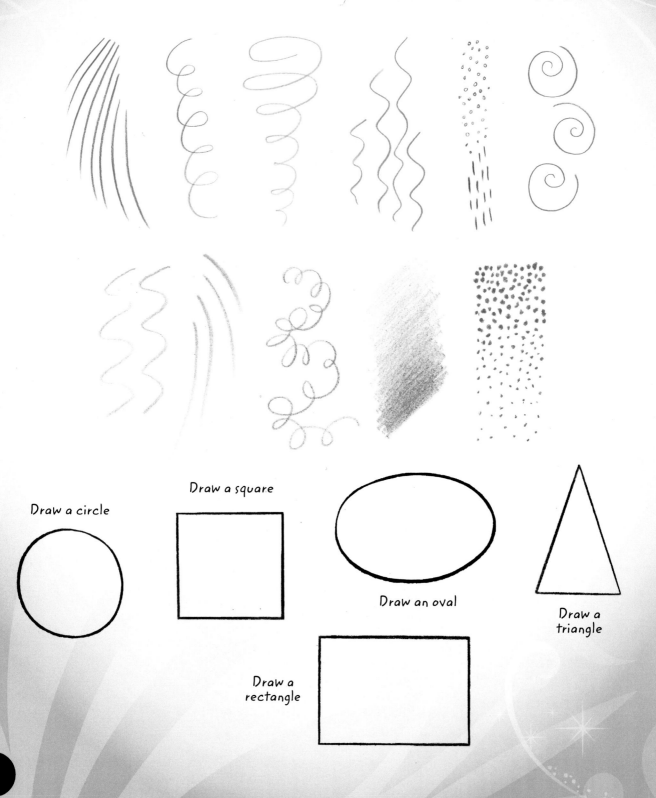

Draw a circle

Draw a square

Draw an oval

Draw a triangle

Draw a rectangle

If you can draw a few basic shapes, you can draw just about anything!

Circle   Carriage   Rectangle   Book

Triangle   Palace   Oval   Teapot   Square   Clock tower

Butterfly   Tiara   Balloon

Gown   Bird

How to Draw
Classic Princesses

Snow White

Snow White is a beautiful young princess who is badly mistreated by her wicked stepmother, the Queen. When creating Snow White, Walt Disney decided to make his first feature princess look more like a pretty "girl next door" than a glamorous princess. Snow White does have rose-red lips, ebony hair, and skin as white as snow that win her the title of "fairest one of all." But her rounded face and figure also show her youth and innocence.

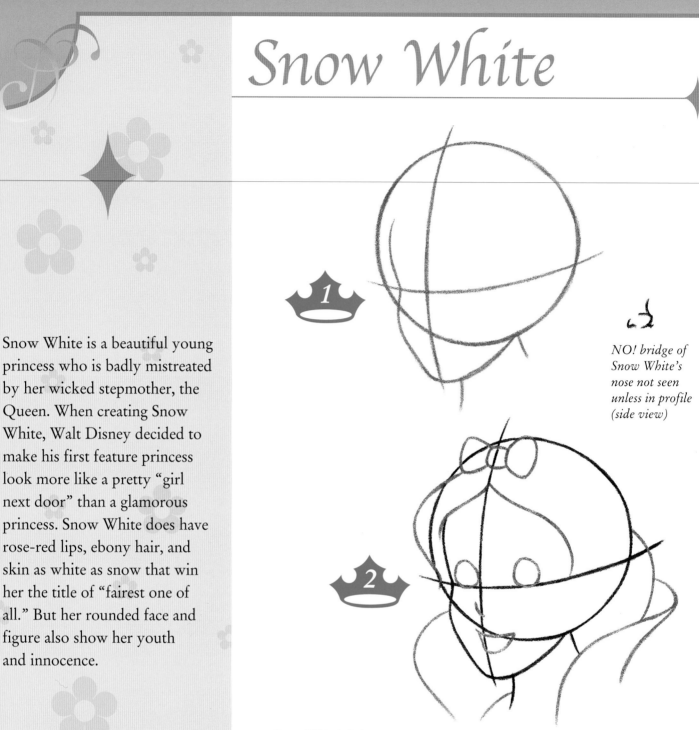

NO! bridge of Snow White's nose not seen unless in profile (side view)

Snow White's hair is drawn with soft curves

eyelashes curl out from her eyelids

top lip is thinner than bottom lip

lips are soft and not too full

3

4

1

3/4

1/2

1/4

0

Snow White's features follow these guidelines

Snow White

Even when she's abandoned in the forest, Snow White's kindness shines through and wins her the friendship of all the forest animals—as well as the love and loyalty of the Seven Dwarfs. When you draw Snow White, be sure to show the soft, sweeping lines in her dress and the gentle arm movements that emphasize her cheerful, sweet disposition and her joy for life.

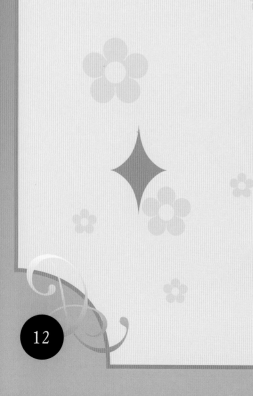

Snow White's hands are rounded and soft like this . . .

. . . not sharp and pointed like this

draw the legs as a guide, even though they're covered by skirt

YES! skirt is wider than hips

NO! skirt is too close to hips

feet are small and delicate

Snow White
is about 6
heads tall

lines are graceful, with
no sharp angles

NO! not angular

figure is
rounded

NO! not
too curvy

Cinderella

Cinderella's story seems much like Snow White's at first. She is treated badly by her stepfamily, but she overcomes all to win the love of a prince. She is also as pretty as can be, whether she appears as a simple house maiden with her hair pulled back or as a glamorous ball guest with her hair swept up.

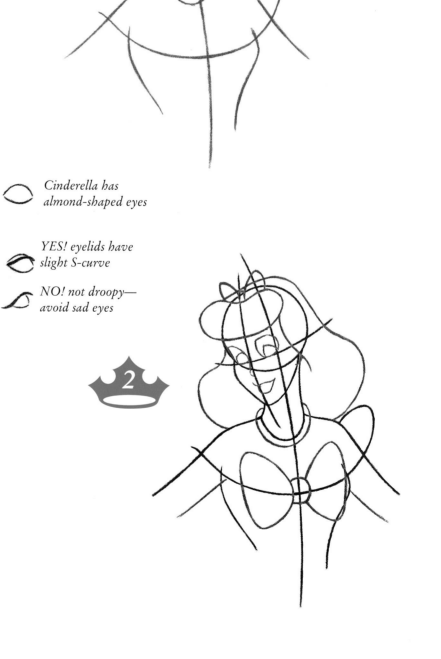

Cinderella has almond-shaped eyes

YES! eyelids have slight S-curve

NO! not droopy— avoid sad eyes

YES! just slight
suggestion of nose

NO! nose is not a
full shape

Cinderella

Cinderella is a very different kind of princess than Snow White. Whereas Snow White wishes and waits for her love to appear, Cinderella wills her dreams to come true, and she goes to find her Prince Charming at the ball.

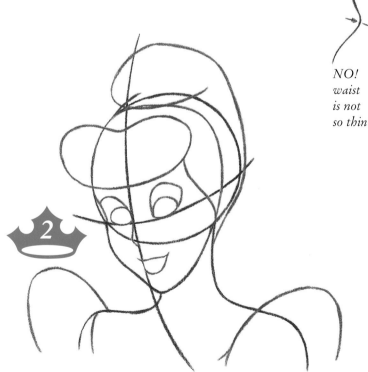

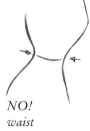

YES! Cinderella's waist is full but not too plump

NO! waist is not so thin

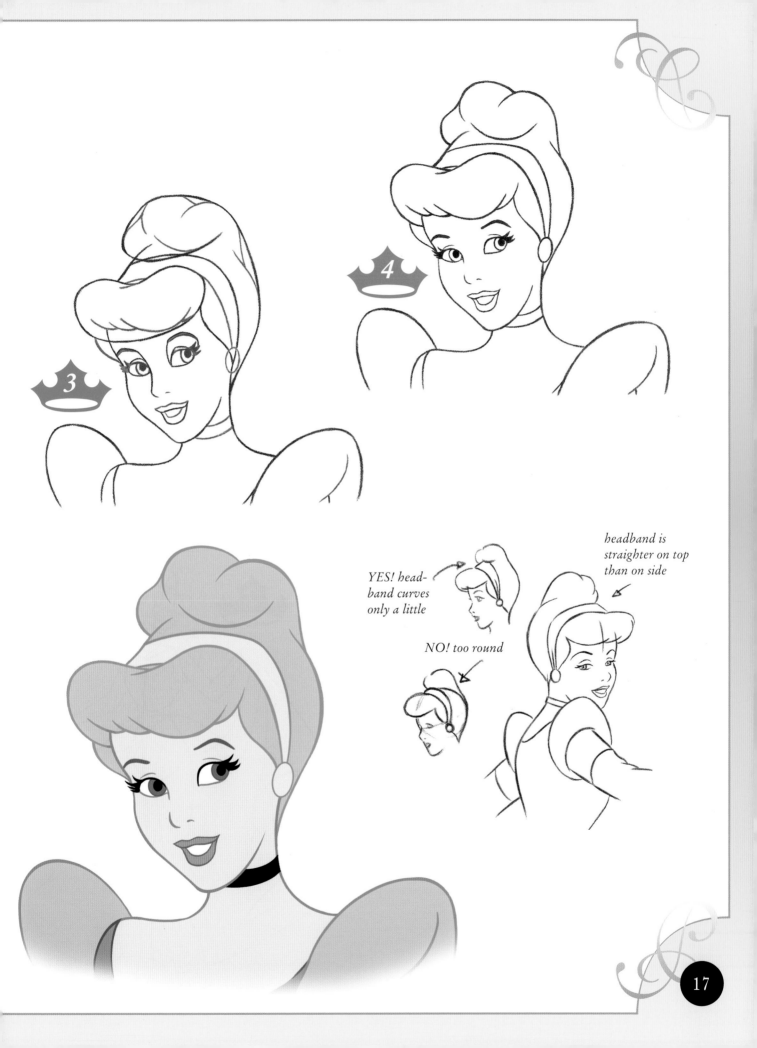

YES! head-
band curves
only a little

headband is
straighter on top
than on side

NO! too round

Cinderella

Cinderella's beauty and graceful movements are evident as she runs down the stairs in her simple, homemade gown, but they become even more obvious at the ball. When she first arrives in her gorgeous dress (thanks to her Fairy Godmother), she immediately attracts everyone's attention, including Prince Charming's. When you draw her sweeping gown with billowing curves, show just a bit of the elegant lace underneath.

Cinderella's fingers are long and slender

YES! angles are soft and smooth

NO! angles are not sharp

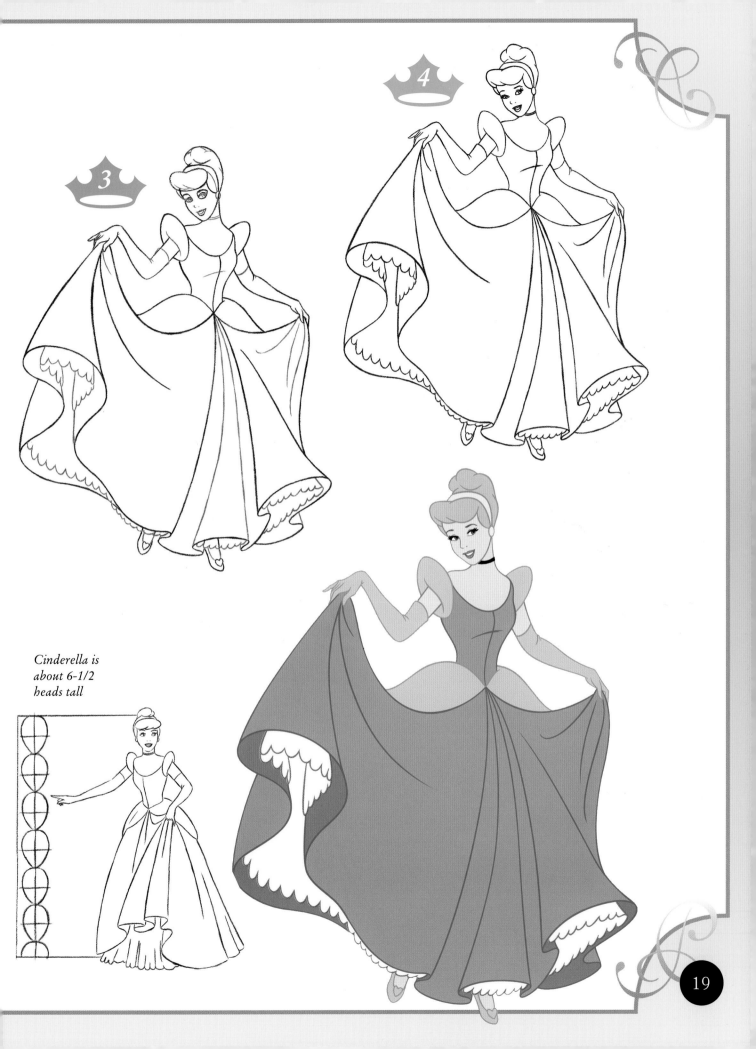

Cinderella is about 6-1/2 heads tall

Sleeping Beauty

Though 16-year-old Princess Aurora has been gifted with beauty, she looks very different from both Snow White and Cinderella. She appears older—more like a woman than like a young girl. Princess Aurora spends the early years of her life in the forest as the "peasant" Briar Rose, where she wears a simple dress and holds back her wavy, waist-length hair with a headband. This is how she looks when she first meets Prince Phillip.

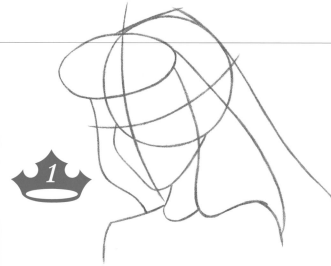

1

2

YES! Sleeping Beauty's hair extends behind head at an angle

NO! not straight down the back of head

eyes tilt up slightly

YES! eyes end in pointed corners and have one thick eyelash

NO! not round— don't draw individual lashes

top of head is
fairly flat   point here

Sleeping Beauty's
features are more
angular than
Snow White's or
Cinderella's

3

4

Sleeping Beauty

Sleeping Beauty's hair curls like this at the back

When Aurora is awakened from her sleep by a kiss from Prince Phillip, she is saved from the curse placed upon her at birth—and she gets to marry her true love! Now when she dances with her prince in the palace, her simple dress is exchanged for a lovely gown, and a beautiful tiara replaces her plain headband. Use long, slightly curved lines for her skirt to show how regal this princess has become.

when she dances, hair swings out like this

3

4

Sleeping Beauty is about 6-1/2 heads tall

waist is very slim

large bangs on the left

big curl on the right

YES! curls are closed, like this

NO! curls are not open

How to Draw

THE
PRINCESS
AND THE
FROG

On a balmy New Orleans evening, two girls listen intently to their favorite fairytale about a frog who needs a princess's kiss to become a prince again. Charlotte says she would kiss a frog in a heartbeat if she could marry a prince. But Tiana says she would never kiss a frog! She has other plans.

Tiana's father, James, shares his dream of opening his own restaurant one day with Tiana. He encourages Tiana to wish upon the Evening Star, but he adds that it will take hard work to make her dreams come true.

The years go by, and Tiana works day and night, saving all of her money to open up her father's dream restaurant. And when the fun-loving, carefree Prince Naveen of Maldonia arrives in New Orleans, Charlotte finally sees an opportunity to marry a prince.

However, the evil voodoo man, Dr. Facilier, has his own plans for Naveen and Naveen's disgruntled valet, Lawrence. Facilier promises Lawrence a princely lifestyle and Naveen a chance to live a carefree life. However, with a handshake to seal the deal, Facilier fulfills his promises in a very unexpected and unfortunate way. With the magic of a talisman, he turns the prince into a frog and Lawrence into the form of Naveen. Then Facilier makes another deal with Lawrence: In return for Naveen's good looks and royal status, Lawrence will marry Charlotte and hand over a large percentage of her fortune to him.

Charlotte's father, Eli "Big Daddy" LaBouff, hosts an extravagant masquerade ball at his mansion. During the ball, Charlotte meets "Prince Naveen" (the transformed Lawrence) while Tiana meets and is instantly repulsed by the real Naveen—in his frog form. When Tiana reluctantly kisses Naveen, something unexpected happens…she transforms into a frog herself!

Both frogs flee to the bayou where they meet a trumpet-playing alligator named Louis and a helpful firefly named Ray. Louis and Ray help Tiana and Naveen escape from frog hunters and get to the powerful priestess Mama Odie. They hope Mama Odie can use her good magic to transform them back into humans. During their journey, Naveen teaches Tiana how to have fun, and Tiana teaches Naveen how to work hard. They finally begin to understand and appreciate one another.

Mama Odie explains that knowing what you need is more important than knowing what you want. Tiana fails to understand Mama Odie's important lesson. Naveen, however, starts to understand. As he looks at Tiana, he begins to realize that she is what he truly needs.

Knowing the two frogs have to figure things out for themselves, Mama Odie instructs Naveen to kiss Charlotte, the "princess" of Mardi Gras, before midnight. Then both frogs will become human again.

When Tiana isn't looking, Facilier's evil shadows swoop down and take Naveen prisoner. Facilier needs Naveen to keep his magical talisman working on Lawrence. Naveen manages to escape and climbs to the top of the Mardi Gras float to expose Lawrence and get to Charlotte. Ray snatches up the talisman and takes it to Tiana. But Facilier shows up and steps on Ray. Having run off with the talisman, Tiana is unaware that Ray is hurt. Facilier quickly tracks down Tiana and corners her. He uses his magic to create a mirage of her dream restaurant and her father. Facilier says she can give her daddy everything he ever wanted—all she has to do is hand over the talisman.

"My Daddy never did get what he wanted, but he had what he needed. He had love," Tiana says. She smashes the talisman to the ground. The shadows descend upon Facilier and he vanishes into thin air, never to be seen again.

Naveen promises to marry Charlotte if she kisses him, but she must help Tiana buy the restaurant. Naveen and Tiana confess their love for each other. Upon hearing this, Charlotte agrees to kiss Naveen—not for herself but for Tiana.

But the clock strikes midnight, and it is too late. Charlotte is no longer the "princess" of Mardi Gras, so Naveen and Tiana both remain frogs. But Naveen and Tiana couldn't be happier because they're together and they're in love. Louis shows up carrying a very weak Ray. Everyone huddles around the firefly as his light flickers out for the last time.

Filled with grief, Tiana, Naveen, and Louis take Ray home to the bayou. They place him in a small leaf boat and let him disappear into the mist. Moments later, a new star shines besides the Evening Star. Ray is finally with his Evangeline.

Soon thereafter, the two frogs get married in the bayou, and they kiss. Then, in a swirl of magic, they become human! As soon as Naveen married Tiana, she became a princess—and with her kiss they both became human again.

After their wedding, Tiana and Naveen open up "Tiana's Palace"—Tiana's dream restaurant. The restaurant is everything that Tiana ever wanted, and her true love is everything she ever needed.

Tiana

Tiana grows up to be an intelligent, beautiful, hardworking young woman, and a very talented cook. She works several waitress jobs and saves every penny. Although her friends often invite her out on the town, she always turns them down. Tiana won't stop working until she has enough money to open the restaurant that she and her father had always dreamed of.

head shape resembles an egg

1

2

3

YES! large, rounder eyes

NO! too narrow

YES! ears are small and rounded

NO! too pointy

"Tiana is the same person throughout. She just literally changes her skin or body. She has similar mannerisms and expressions as a human and as a frog. I never looked at them differently."
—Mark Henn, Disney animator

4

masquerade
ball tiara

nose is short
and round

rounded
chin

Princess Tiana

When Tiana marries Naveen, she not only regains her human form,
she becomes a princess! Tiana finally gets her dream restaurant
and finds true love with her prince!

Tiana has
dimples on
her cheeks

nose is about
same width as
the distance
between eyes

narrow wrists

Tiana's bayou wedding crown is made of petals and stamens of varying shapes and sizes.

3

4

full bottom lip

©Disney

Tiana the frog

Being green isn't easy! When Tiana is transformed into a frog, she's faced with brand new challenges: finding her way through the bayou, escaping from frog hunters, and catching flies with her long, sticky tongue! But even as a frog, Tiana proves that she's very capable and hardworking. Whether it's making a boat on which to float down the bayou or whipping up a batch of gumbo for her friends, Tiana can get things done.

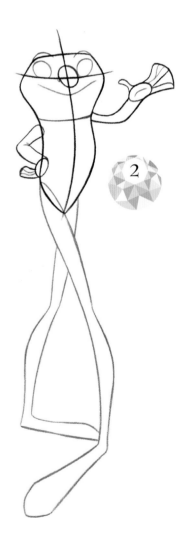

1

2

Tiana's eyes are one eye's width apart

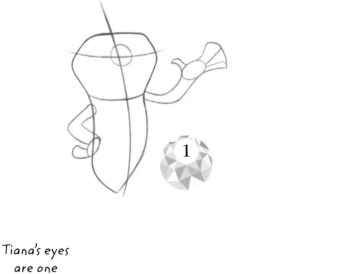

full lashes

eyebrow

eyelid

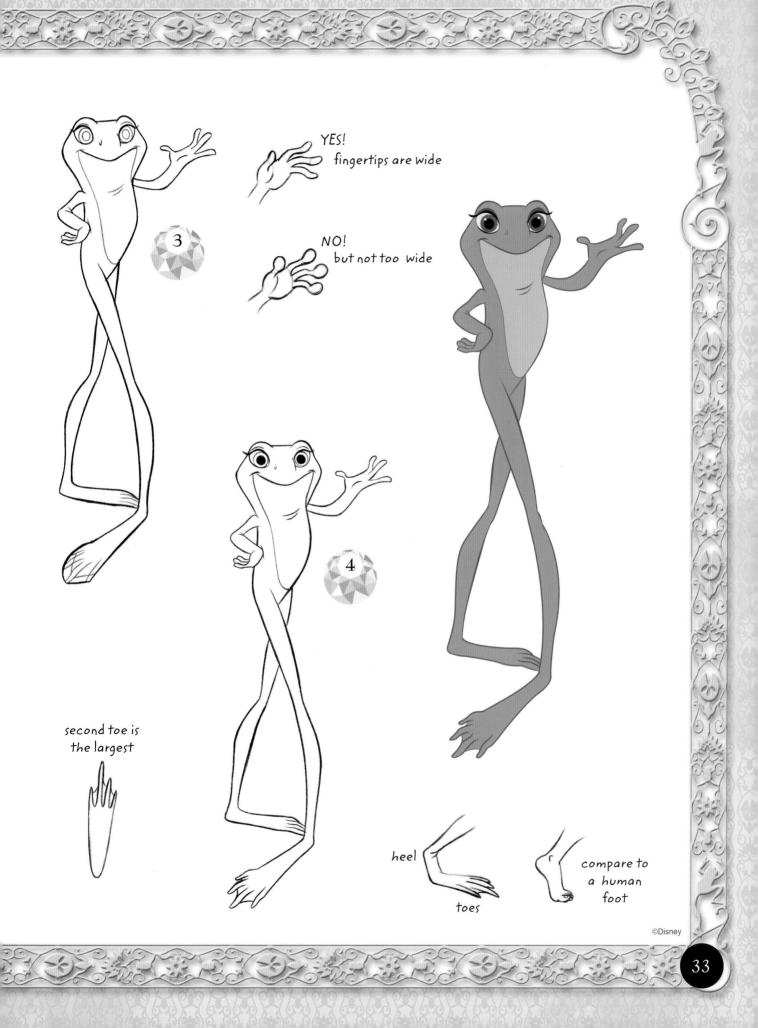

YES!
fingertips are wide

NO!
but not too wide

3

4

second toe is
the largest

heel

toes

compare to
a human
foot

©Disney

Naveen

Naveen is the handsome, free-spirited, and fun-loving prince from the country of Maldonia. He's a jazz fanatic and has traveled to New Orleans—the birthplace of jazz—to sing, dance, and play to his heart's content. But Naveen's carefree and irresponsible ways have caused his parents to cut him off. Now he's faced with his most dreaded fear: having to work for a living.

YES!   NO!

nose curves out, not in

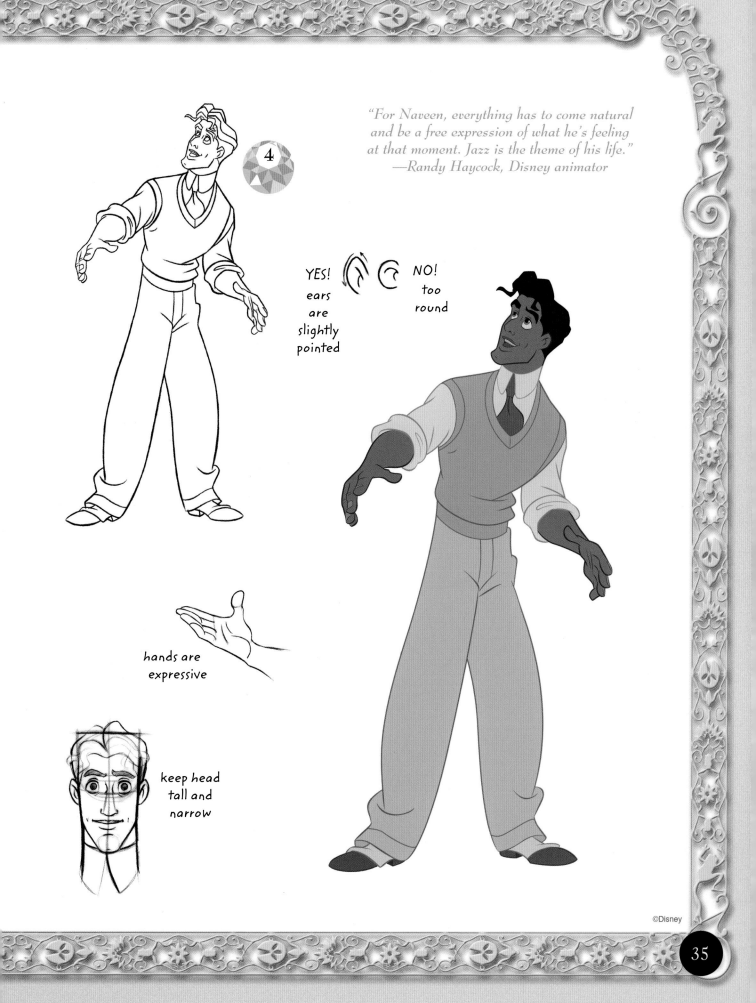

"For Naveen, everything has to come natural
and be a free expression of what he's feeling
at that moment. Jazz is the theme of his life."
—Randy Haycock, Disney animator

4

YES!
ears
are
slightly
pointed

NO!
too
round

hands are
expressive

keep head
tall and
narrow

Naveen the frog

When Facilier uses his talisman to cast a spell on Naveen, the prince transforms into a frog. But even in his new amphibious form, Naveen isn't much different. He floats down the bayou river, lounges about, and plays jazz. But when Tiana teaches him a few things about responsibility and hard work, his views begin to change.

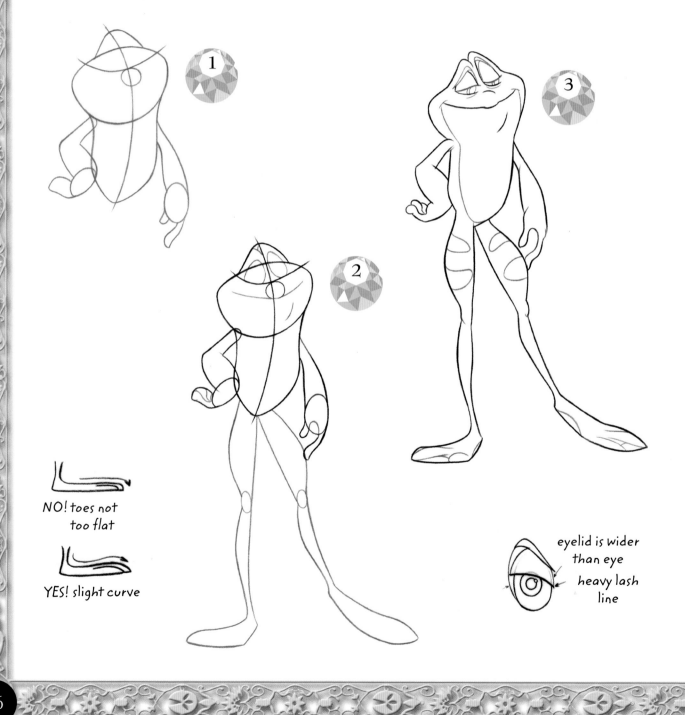

1

2

3

NO! toes not
too flat

YES! slight curve

eyelid is wider
than eye

heavy lash
line

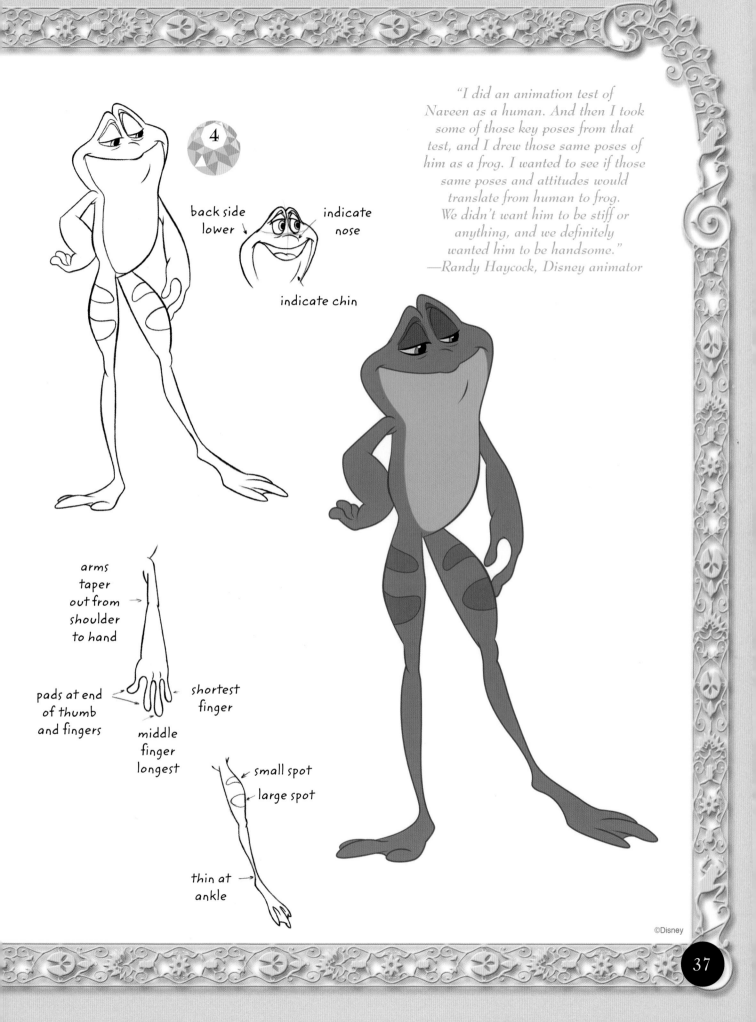

4

back side lower →

indicate nose

indicate chin

"I did an animation test of Naveen as a human. And then I took some of those key poses from that test, and I drew those same poses of him as a frog. I wanted to see if those same poses and attitudes would translate from human to frog. We didn't want him to be stiff or anything, and we definitely wanted him to be handsome."
—Randy Haycock, Disney animator

arms taper out from shoulder to hand →

pads at end of thumb and fingers →

shortest finger

middle finger longest

small spot

large spot

thin at ankle →

Louis

Louis is a huge alligator who knows all about jazz, having listened to the great jazz musicians perform on the riverboats passing through the bayou. When he found a discarded trumpet (which he named Giselle), Louis taught himself to play and became a true jazz master himself. His dream is to play for a human audience while not scaring them half to death.

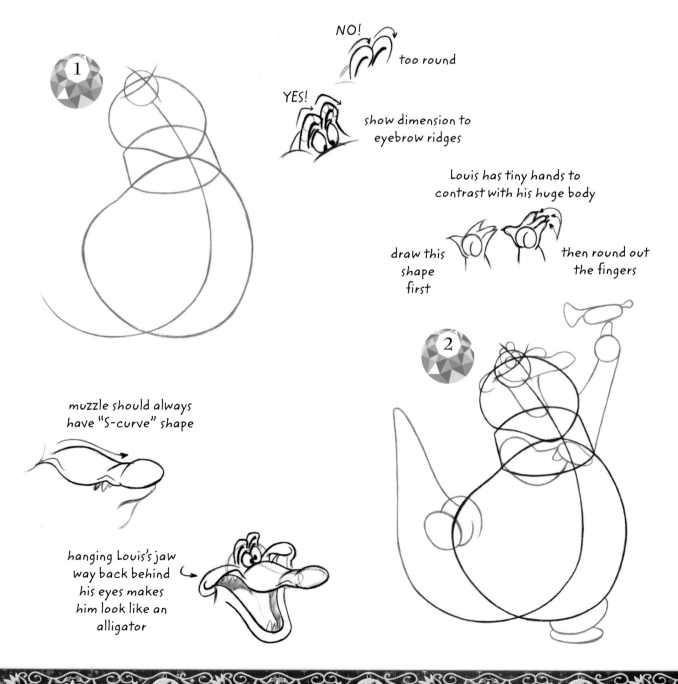

NO!

too round

YES!

show dimension to eyebrow ridges

Louis has tiny hands to contrast with his huge body

draw this shape first

then round out the fingers

muzzle should always have "S-curve" shape

hanging Louis's jaw way back behind his eyes makes him look like an alligator

3

4

pupil can protrude off
the whites

"Louis is generally a bundle of
nerves in a gator suit…however,
Louis has a heart as big as his
girth, which he reveals most
successfully when blowing his
trumpet. Louis's big dream is to
play jazz 'with the big boys' in the
human world. Now, if it weren't
for all those teeth…"
—Eric Goldberg, Disney animator

Ray

Ray is a lovesick Cajun firefly who's constantly pining for his beloved Evangeline—
the Evening Star, whom he believes is a firefly. Even though he and Evangeline are
from separate worlds, Ray believes love conquers all. Someday they will be together.
Ray is also a loyal and courageous friend. He may be small, but he's also mighty!
And he's always there to help his friends when they need him.

*"When drawing Ray, make sure you
have a sense of rhythm. Allow one
shape to flow naturally into the next."*
—Mike Surrey, Disney animator

don't make
chin too round

← YES!

← NO!

40

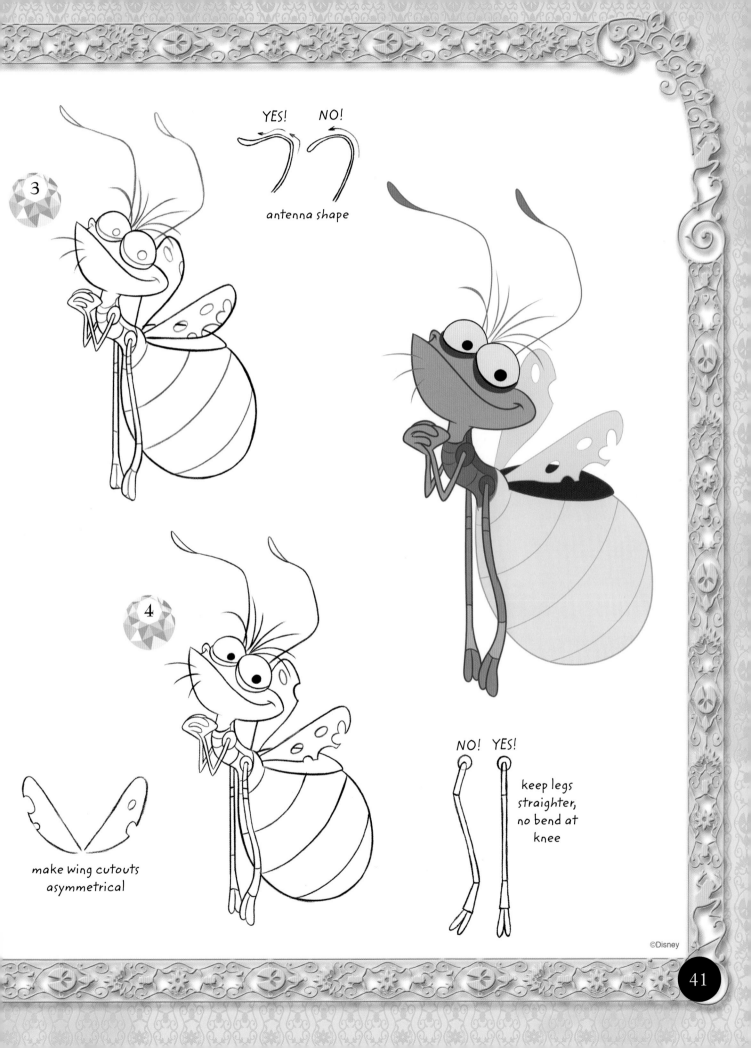

3

YES!   NO!

antenna shape

4

make wing cutouts
asymmetrical

NO! YES!

keep legs
straighter,
no bend at
knee

How to Draw

THE LITTLE MERMAID

Ariel

The three-quarter view is the best angle to use to make a character look three-dimensional. Notice how much depth, form, and structure can be achieved in this drawing of Ariel's head.

4

5

6

People around the world have been charmed by Ariel's cheerful enthusiasm.
Be sure to show some of her energy when drawing her complete figure.
A strong line of action will help give the feeling that Ariel's body flows
naturally into her graceful tail!

NO!

YES!

give her tail natural-
looking movement

4

5

Ariel is
6 heads tall

Ariel is so excited to become a human and try out her new legs.
She hopes Prince Eric will notice her without her voice, so make sure
her very first gown is fit for a beautiful princess!

NO!
hand does not
point down

6

7

52

8

Prince Eric

Eric's handsome looks capture Ariel's heart so much that she is willing to change her whole life to be with him. Make sure you draw him standing proudly, like the strong prince he is.

Sebastian

Sebastian is a little crab with a big voice and a big heart. Try to bring out the warmer side of his personality when you draw him.

Sebastian is
6 heads tall

6

7

8

57

Flounder

Flounder's spunk and vulnerability are the qualities
that make him so memorable. Use this three-quarter view to
show all the depth of his chubby cheeks and oval nose.

6

7

Out →
In →

In →
Out →

8

How to Draw

Beauty and the Beast

The Making of *Beauty and the Beast*

The Disney movie *Beauty and the Beast* opened in 1991 to an eager audience. *The Little Mermaid* had remained enormously popular, and *Beauty and the Beast* promised to be even more so.

Audiences were not disappointed. The Disney artists' dedication and love for their craft ensured that *Beauty and the Beast* would be animation at its best. Early during the production, it was acknowledged that music would be the driving force in the re-telling of this classic tale. Musical numbers that would rival Broadway show-stoppers were composed and integrated into the story. After the directors approved the script and songs, it was time for the artists to get to work. Painstaking efforts produced lavish scenes and hours of research resulting in authentic backgrounds and costumes.

The main characters required the
most intensive research. Belle appears
twice as often as any other character
in the movie, so it was important to
get her look right. She is a natural
beauty—young, but far from naive.
Her healthy coloring comes from
an active life, not
from cosmetics.

Belle's slightly tilted eyes give
her a mature look, especially when
compared to such female characters as
Wendy from *Peter Pan,* or even Cinderella.
Not since *Snow White and the Seven Dwarfs*
had Disney featured a dark-haired heroine.

A very different approach was needed in designing the character of the Beast. Animators studied a variety of wild animals to get a sense of what makes them so fearsome. Early sketches of the Beast show him resembling a mandrill, and later, a buffalo. Study the finished Beast and you will see a little of each—with the addition of a boar's tusks, a bear's body, and a wolf's tail.

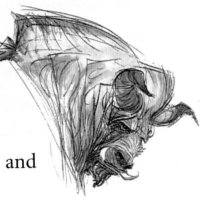

Gaston is easily recognized as an arrogant, conceited male, while his sidekick LeFou (whose name means "the fool" in French) is a hilarious combination of cartoon clowns.

Lumiere, Cogsworth, and Mrs. Potts are more than just household objects. Look carefully at their faces—they are far more human than anything else.

As time goes on, the Disney studios will undoubtedly produce other animated masterpieces. But *Beauty and the Beast,* the "tale as old as time," can never be surpassed in the hearts of the artists who created it.

Belle

In this front view of Belle's head,
notice how soft curves create her simple beauty.

1

2

Belle's eyes are set wide
apart and tilt slightly up.

3

4

5

Belle's Expressions

Belle's love of books makes her yearn for faraway places and adventures.
Knowing her traits will help you draw Belle in a variety of moods
and expressions.

caring

amused

happy

skeptical

surprised

daydreaming

worried

frightened

Belle

Belle is a simple country girl, with a natural beauty that is as much inner goodness as it is looks.

1

2

3

4

Keep Belle very graceful and tall, with a tapered waist and long, slender legs.

5

6

7

Belle Action Poses

Now that you've learned to draw Belle's face and body, you can really bring her to life in these action poses.

73

Lumiere and Cogsworth

Lumiere and Cogsworth have unusual bodies, but they manage to move in a very human fashion. Notice how they use their parts like arms and legs.

Mrs. Potts and Chip

Mrs. Potts is a warmhearted teapot. Chip, a teacup, is like a wide-eyed child. Keep these traits in mind as you draw them in these poses.

The Beast

The Beast is a combination of many wild animals, but underneath that savage exterior is a frightened young man. Follow the steps and see the depth, form, and structure as you draw the Beast's head.

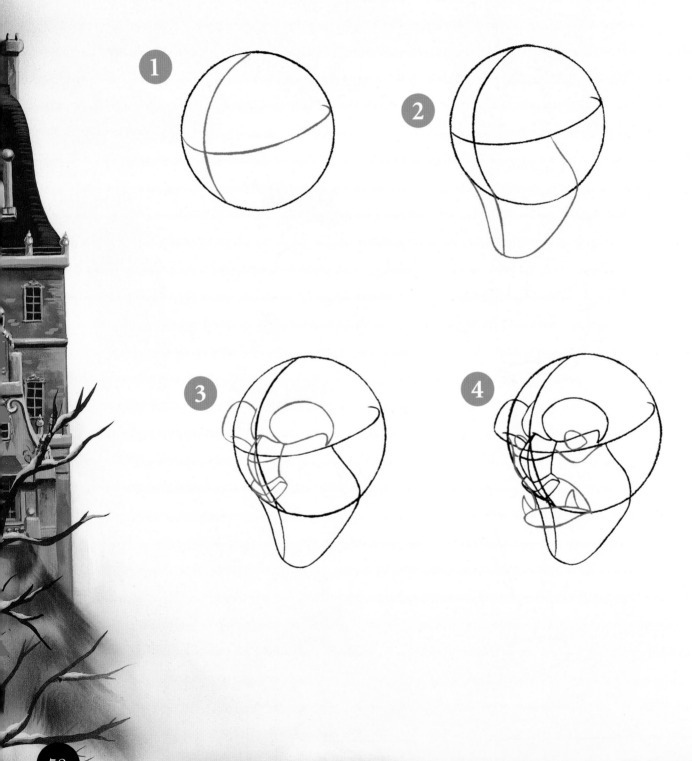

5

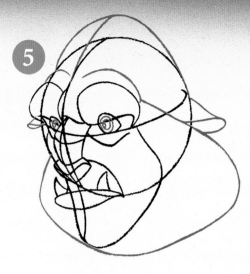

6

Use short, rough strokes for the
Beast's fur, and careful,
detailed lines for his face.

7

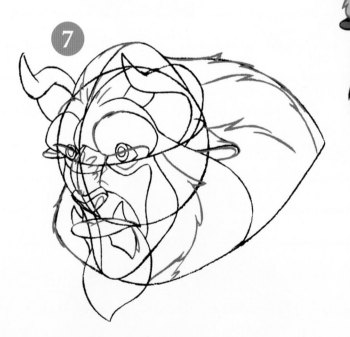

The Beast's Expressions

Even the Beast has feelings! Knowing his personality
will help you make him more believable.

thoughtful

happy

angry

fearful

loving

sad

wounded

sulking

Disney
PRINCESS
How to Draw
Aladdin

The Making of *Aladdin*

The story of Aladdin dates back as far as 850 A.D. and is a compilation of almost 200 folktales from Persian, Indian, and Arabian cultures. Despite this, the Disney studios did not begin working on *Aladdin* until 1990! It may have taken a long time for Disney's version of the story to reach the big screen, but everyone agrees that it was well worth the wait.

Aladdin was a challenge to the Disney artists. Earlier Disney movies were based on European fairy tales and had similar-looking characters and backgrounds. *Aladdin* stretched the artists' imaginations and drawing abilities to the fullest.

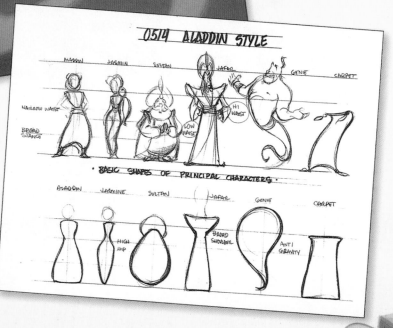

Mysterious Arabian nights and desert dunes replaced sunny meadows and stately forests. Fluffy bunnies and cheerful baby birds are nowhere to be seen. Instead, there are dancing camels, ferocious tigers, and a wise-cracking parrot. The craft of animation took a front seat as the Genie performed amazing transformations at a rapid-fire pace. An exotic feeling prevails in *Aladdin*—the result of intensive research, artistic skill, and countless hours of hard work.

Aladdin himself was the most challenging to design. The success of the movie depended greatly upon his keeping the audience's interest while surrounded by so many flamboyant and compelling co-stars.

In design, Princess Jasmine is very much an Arabian princess. Earlier Disney princesses were European, and wore traditional crowns and long, flowing gowns. Jasmine broke the trend with her light, billowy harem pants and short top.

It took more than 500 dedicated artists to make *Aladdin*. Their talent, humor, and thorough enjoyment of their challenging subject matter are evident in every frame of the film, and all can be proud to have worked on another Disney classic.

Jasmine

The beautiful Princess Jasmine captures the heart of Aladdin. When drawing this three-quarter view, notice how her large brown eyes have a gentle upward slant.

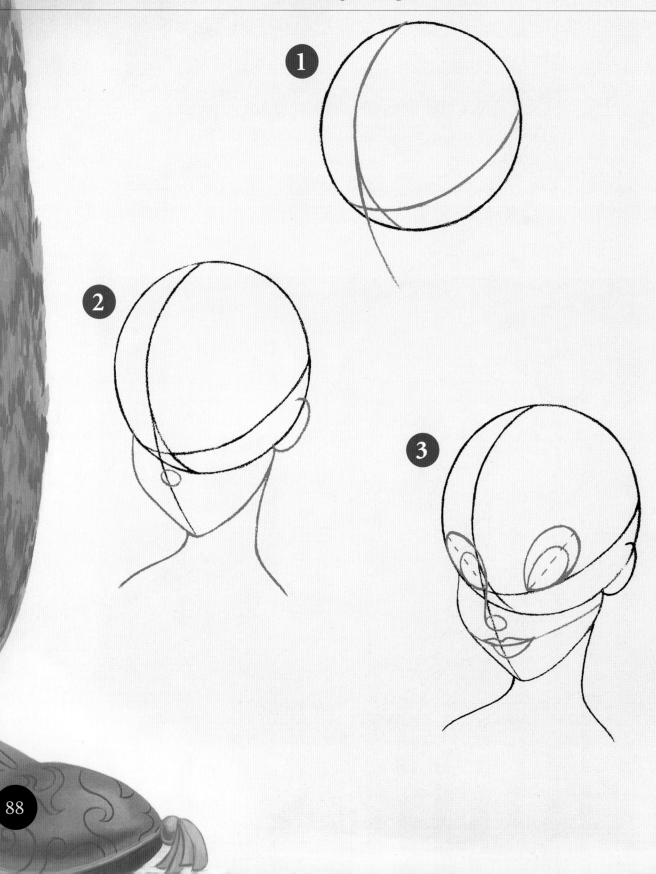

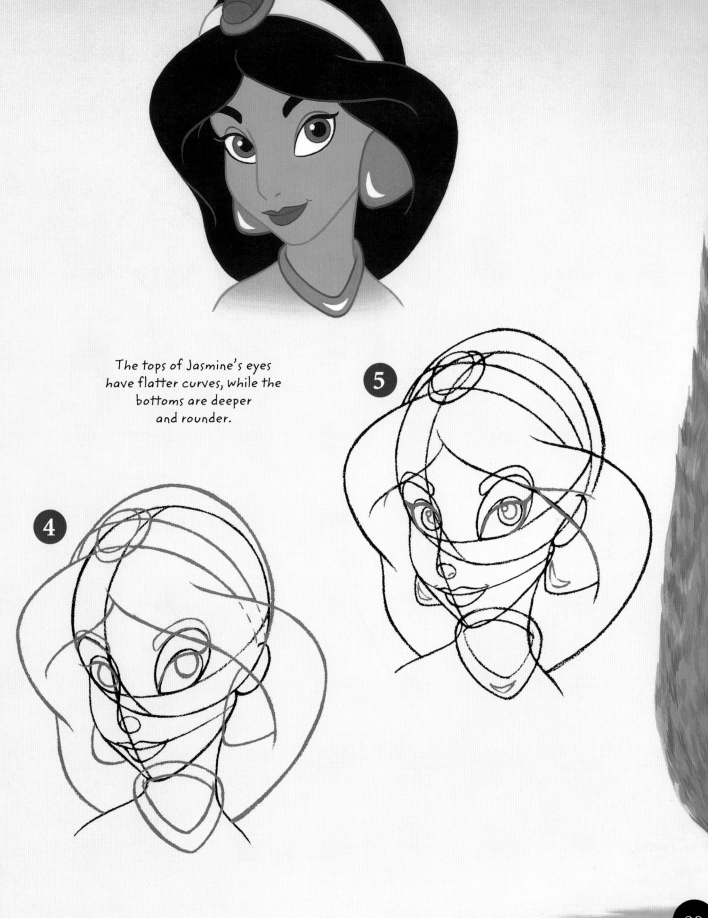

The tops of Jasmine's eyes
have flatter curves, while the
bottoms are deeper
and rounder.

5

4

Jasmine

Jasmine has a slender figure. She carries herself with dignity and grace.

4

Jasmine Action Poses

Jasmine may look delicate, but she is a fiery beauty and can take care of herself. Enhance her personality with the following mannerisms and poses.

The Genie

The Genie's sense of humor is apparent in his wide smile and twinkling eyes.

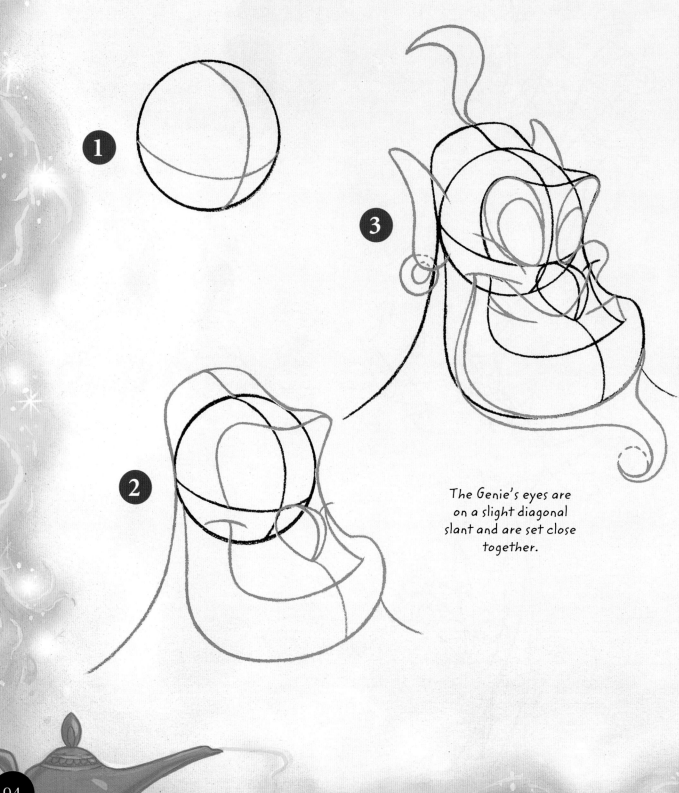

The Genie's eyes are on a slight diagonal slant and are set close together.

4

Don't forget the Genie's earring, and notice how his beard ends in a distinctive spiral.

Aladdin

Aladdin is a dashing young hero with a devil-may-care attitude. Try to capture the depth and form, as shown in the steps below.

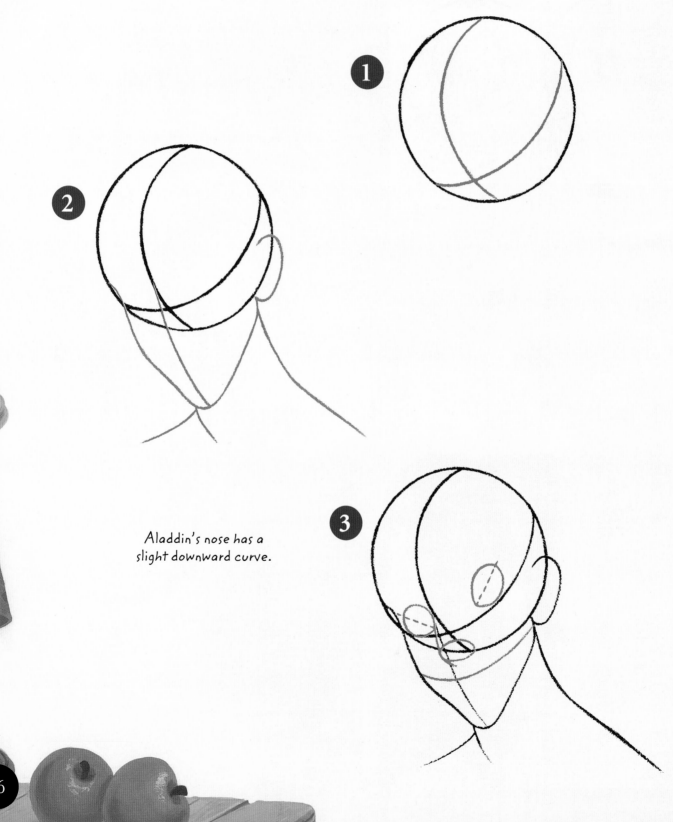

Aladdin's nose has a slight downward curve.

4

Aladdin's hair is widest at eyebrow level.

5

Aladdin

Living on the streets of Agrabah has made Aladdin lean and strong.
Keep his limbs athletic, but not too muscular.

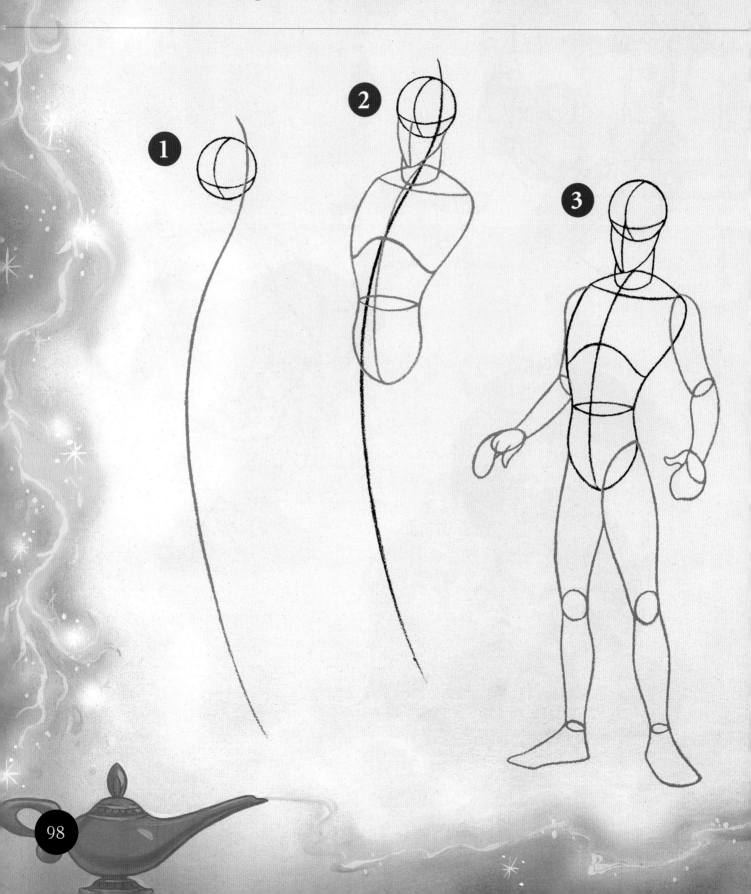

4

5

Aladdin has broad shoulders and a wide stance.

Disney PRINCESS
How to Draw
Tangled

The Story of Tangled

Bells chimed throughout the kingdom; the royal horns blared. At last, the King and Queen stepped proudly out onto the balcony to present their newborn princess. The crowds cheered happily, and as evening settled in, the King and Queen launched a single floating lantern into the sky in celebration.

But all too soon, the happiness ended. A vain, selfish woman named Mother Gothel stole the infant. For Mother Gothel had discovered a secret: The babe's golden hair possessed the magic to heal—and to keep Mother Gothel young and beautiful forever.

And so the princess Rapunzel grew up in a tower hidden in a secret valley. Mother Gothel lied to Rapunzel to keep her from leaving the tower, saying that the world outside was filled with ruffians and thugs who wanted to steal her magical golden hair.

Every year, the kingdom launched a thousand floating lights on the night of the princess's birthday in hopes of guiding her home someday. And every year, Rapunzel watched the lights from the top of the tower, yearning to see them up close.

The day before Rapunzel's 18th birthday, a dashing thief named Flynn Rider was racing through the forest. He'd had quite a day that included stealing the lost princess's crown from the kingdom (something that would bring him a large reward), cutting ties with his cutthroat companions (the Stabbington brothers), and evading the royal guards and all of their horses—except one.

Maximus was the best horse in the royal guard—strong, smart, and relentless. After a wild chase, Flynn escaped the gray and white steed by finding a hidden tunnel that led to a secret valley. In the middle of this beautiful oasis stood a tower.

Flynn climbed up the tower and in through a window at the top. TWANG! Rapunzel knocked him unconscious. She and her best friend, a chameleon named Pascal, hid his satchel that harbored the valuable crown.

Seeing this as her only opportunity to get out of the tower, Rapunzel made a deal with Flynn: he would guide her to see the lights and then return her to the tower before Mother Gothel knew she had left; then she would return his satchel.

And so, with a reluctant thief to guide her, Rapunzel finally slid down her hair and left the tower. She was thrilled with the outside world. It smelled, looked, and felt wonderful!

Rapunzel and Flynn, along with Pascal, embarked on the adventure of their lives, which included evading the palace guards, Maximus, the Stabbington brothers, and even Mother Gothel. All the while, Flynn was shocked to find himself bonded to this courageous, spirited, beautiful girl.

Maximus caught up with Flynn the morning of Rapunzel's birthday. Luckily Rapunzel acted as peacemaker between the two—nothing would keep her from seeing the floating lights up close!

After enjoying a fun-filled day in the kingdom, that evening Rapunzel finally found her dream in a sky filled with floating lanterns—and in Flynn's eyes. They were falling in love. Nothing could stop them—except Mother Gothel.

With the help of the Stabbington brothers, Mother Gothel set up Flynn and sent him to the palace jail; then she tricked Rapunzel into believing Flynn had left her. Feeling broken-hearted and betrayed, Rapunzel returned to the tower with Mother Gothel. Luckily, Maximus orchestrated a plan to help Flynn escape. Together he and Flynn galloped off to save Rapunzel.

"Rapunzel!" Flynn yelled from the base of the tower. "Rapunzel, let down your hair!" The golden hair unfurled and Flynn climbed up, but Mother Gothel was waiting for him. She wounded him gravely. Rapunzel, who was tied up, begged to heal Flynn with the power of her magic hair. But Mother Gothel would not let Rapunzel near him—unless she promised to stay in the tower forever and never try to run away again. Rapunzel gave her word.

Just before Rapunzel could heal him, Flynn cut her hair. Once cut, the golden locks lost their power. Mother Gothel aged hundreds of years and faded away.

As Flynn closed his eyes, Rapunzel wept. A single golden tear fell upon Flynn's cheek. His eyes fluttered open. The magic was inside of Rapunzel all along. He was healed!

With Maximus and Pascal, Rapunzel and Flynn returned to the kingdom. Overjoyed, the King and Queen embraced their long-lost daughter. It was a love Rapunzel had never felt from Mother Gothel. It was true love.

Rapunzel was home at last.

Rapunzel

Rapunzel may have grown up in a tower, but she is full of energy, which she uses to take care of her hair that grows and grows and grows! Her days are filled with many things, including reading, cooking, and painting. Her beautiful art covers the walls and the ceiling of the tower. When drawing Rapunzel, don't forget to think of her spirit and her curiosity about the world outside. Even though she could not leave the tower, she dreamed big!

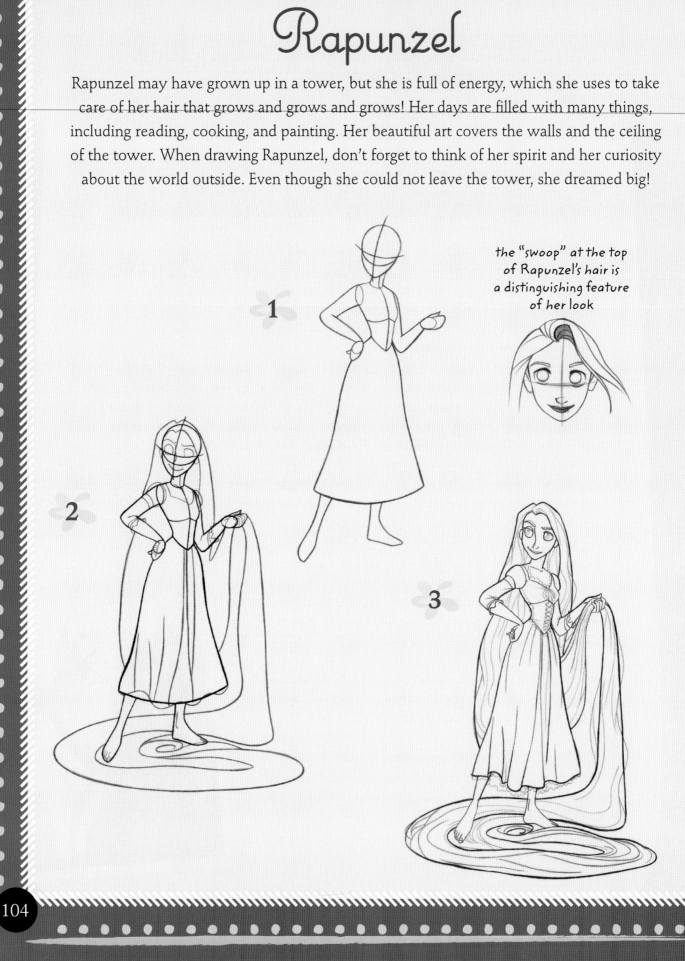

1

the "swoop" at the top of Rapunzel's hair is a distinguishing feature of her look

2

3

Rapunzel's hair has a lot of weight that forms simple shapes

4

NO!

YES!

hair has volume and thickness, even when lying on the floor

Princess Rapunzel

Even after Flynn cuts Rapunzel's hair, she remains the spirited young woman she has always been. Being reunited with her parents is a joy, and she cannot believe how amazing the world outside the tower is!

4

after Rapunzel's hair is
cut, it turns brown and
maintains soft waves along
the bottom edges

Flynn Rider

Flynn Rider is a thief. Handsome, charismatic, and slightly vain, he fancies himself rather charming with the women. But he meets his match with Rapunzel. Through the amazing adventure they share together, he decides to change his ways, give up thievery, and become a nice guy.

4

Flynn's shoulders are about twice as wide as his hips

Flynn is about 6-1/2 heads tall

Pascal

Pascal is Rapunzel's best friend. The friendly chameleon has a way of understanding whatever Rapunzel is feeling—and he reflects it by changing color and expressions. She shares her innermost secrets with him, and she never has to worry that he will tell anyone!

tail can unroll
to express emotion

1

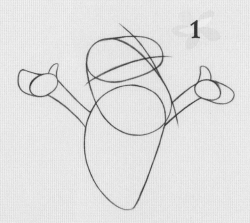

2

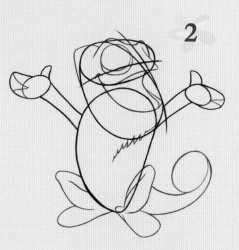

3

4

feet have 3 toes

careful with the
shape of the head

NO!   YES!

not like a shark fin   a bit rounded

How to Draw

DISNEY · PIXAR

BRAVE

Merida is the adventurous Princess of DunBroch, who is more comfortable shooting her bow than wearing ball gowns. Independent and feisty, Merida is horrified that her parents have invited the lords of three neighboring clans to bring their sons to the castle for a competition—where the prize is Merida's hand in marriage!

Determined to avoid the fate that awaits her, Merida defies this age-old tradition and instead participates in the archery competition to win her own hand in marriage. She shoots all three bullseyes to win the competition, but her defiance causes a ruckus in the kingdom and an argument with her mother. Merida runs away and rides into the forest on her horse, Angus. She soon comes across a witch who gives her a spell cake that, Merida hopes, will change her mother's mind about the princess's marriage.

As soon as Elinor eats the cake, she is transformed into a bear. As Merida and Elinor fight to transform Elinor back into the queen she is, they embark on a journey of bravery to prove that love can beat all odds.

MERIDA

Merida is adventurous and athletic, and she loves to be outdoors in the sunshine.
Make sure to give her movement and a free-spirited look in your drawing.

for Merida's hair, use wild, squiggly lines

eyes and brows are more round

NO!   YES!

MERIDA IN ACTION

Fergus and Elinor invited the lords of the Highland clans to present their sons as suitors in a competition to win Merida's hand in marriage. In a demonstration of courage and skill, Merida takes matters into her own hands—she hits each bullseye herself, winning the competition and successfully defending her independence.

profile is curvy

small nose

ELINOR THE BEAR

Even when Elinor is transformed into a bear, she still has mannerisms and poses that hint at her true identity as queen. Try to show the human emotion she feels during this adventure with her daughter in your drawing.

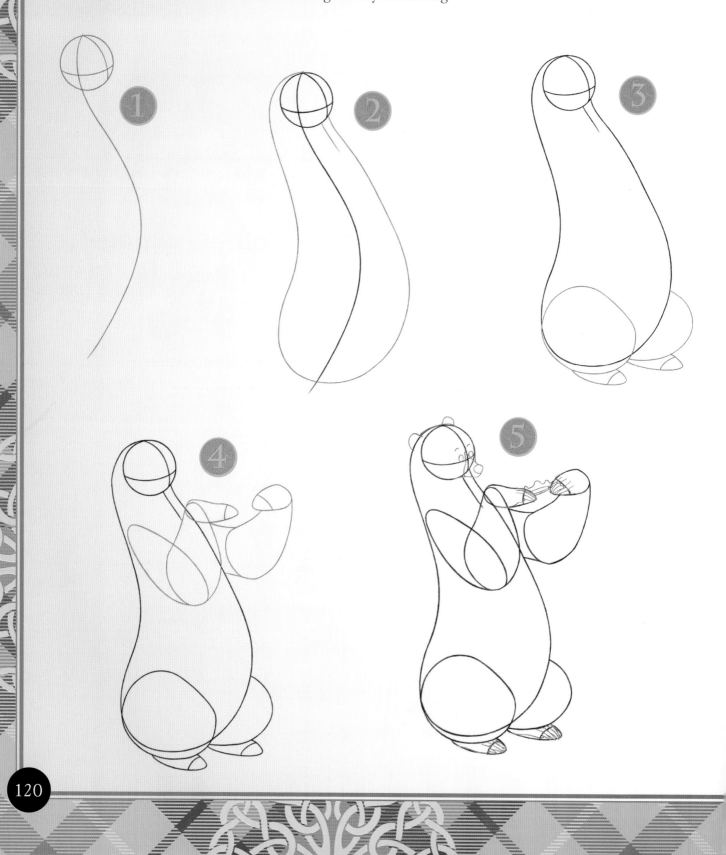

NO! not spaced too evenly

YES! five claws grouped together

NO! not pointy

YES! ears rounded

6

7

121

How to Draw

MULAN

The Making of Mulan

When we first meet Mulan, she is struggling mightily to assume the traditional role of a Chinese woman to please her father, whom she loves dearly. But her high spirits and bold approach get in the way. In designing Mulan's image, Disney artists focused on graceful, flowing shapes for her dark hair, her slightly angled eyes, and her athletic figure. Her feminine face is free of distracting details, yet her passionate spirit shines through.

Mulan's individuality—and the antics of her "lucky" cricket, Cri-Kee—make a disaster out of her meeting with the Matchmaker. Feeling responsible, Cri-Kee tries to redeem himself by bringing Mulan the good fortune he symbolizes. Her tiny companion cannot speak, so animators had to convey Cri-Kee's thoughts through his expressive eyes and poses.

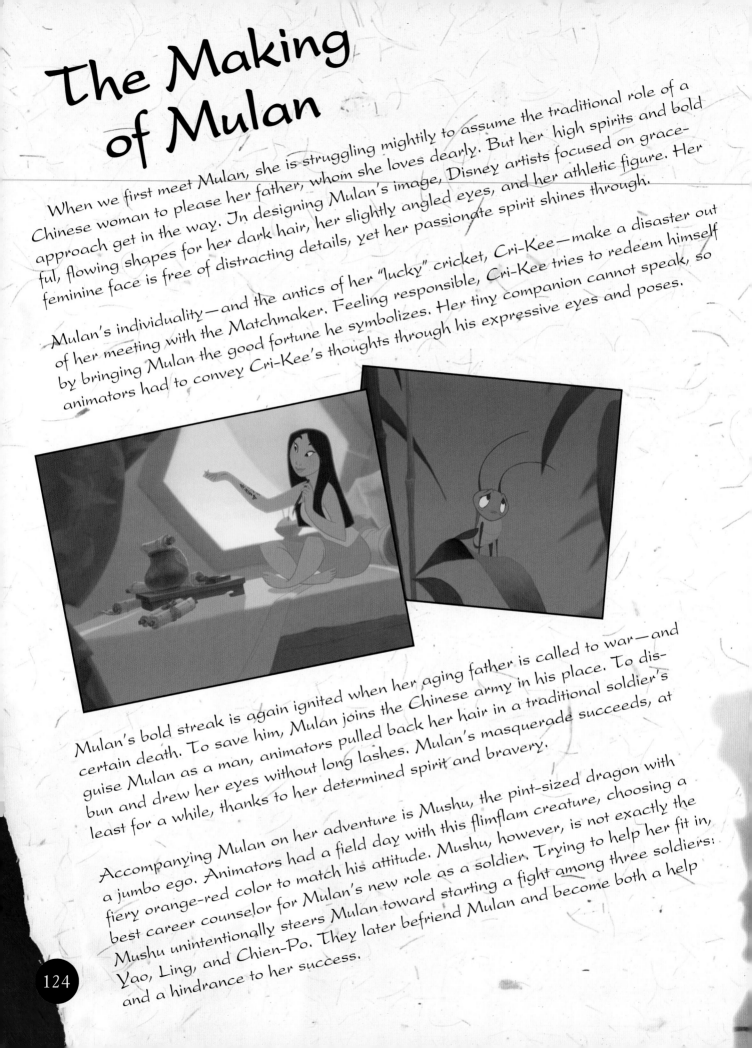

Mulan's bold streak is again ignited when her aging father is called to war—and certain death. To save him, Mulan joins the Chinese army in his place. To disguise Mulan as a man, animators pulled back her hair in a traditional soldier's bun and drew her eyes without long lashes. Mulan's masquerade succeeds, at least for a while, thanks to her determined spirit and bravery.

Accompanying Mulan on her adventure is Mushu, the pint-sized dragon with a jumbo ego. Animators had a field day with this flimflam creature, choosing a fiery orange-red color to match his attitude. Mushu, however, is not exactly the best career counselor for Mulan's new role as a soldier. Trying to help her fit in, Mushu unintentionally steers Mulan toward starting a fight among three soldiers: Yao, Ling, and Chien-Po. They later befriend Mulan and become both a help and a hindrance to her success.

These three almost discover Mulan's real identity when they join her—uninvited—for a bath in the lake. Her faithful horse, Khan, comes to her rescue, shielding Mulan from view as she exits the lake. Animators based Khan on a Tang Dynasty horse, giving him a powerful body with a calligraphic feel.

Unfortunately, Mulan's deception is discovered when she is wounded in battle. Because Captain Li Shang, commander of the troops, feels betrayed by her, Mulan and her companions, Cri-Kee, Mushu, and Khan, are left behind when Shang moves his troops out. But when she discovers that the terrible enemy Shan-Yu has survived and is proceeding toward the Imperial City, Mulan rises to the occasion yet again. Her ingenuity helps her defeat the Hun invaders once and for all. She saves the Emperor, earning Shang's respect and bringing honor to her beloved parents. The heroine of Walt Disney Pictures' 36th full-length animated feature film, Mulan shows how great things can be accomplished through sheer determination, grace, and a great deal of heart.

Mulan

THIS PLUCKY HEROINE IS A STUDY IN CONTRASTS. MULAN IS GRACEFUL, YET FEISTY; RESPECTFUL, YET DEFIANT. BEHIND HER CLASSIC ASIAN FEATURES LIES A QUICK MIND—AND SHE'S NOT AFRAID TO SPEAK IT. ANIMATORS HAD TO SHOW BOTH THE OUTWARDLY TRADITIONAL MULAN AND HER BOLD INNER SPIRIT. THEY CHOSE TO CREATE HER CHARACTER USING SIMPLE SHAPES AND FEW DETAILS. HER CLEAN, DOWN-TO-EARTH LOOK EMPHASIZES THAT SHE JUST WANTS TO BE TRUE TO HERSELF. AS YOU DRAW MULAN, FOCUS ON SIMPLICITY, SHAPE, AND PROPORTION.

HAIR WILL FAVOR ONE SIDE OR OTHER, DEPENDING ON TURN OF HEAD

EYE LINE HALFWAY

1/2

1/2

EGG-SHAPED (OVAL) HEAD

LID IS PARALLEL TO LASH

MOUTH IS WIDER THAN NOSE

NOSE SHOULD BE HALF WAY BETWEEN EYE LINE AND CHIN

BASIC EYE SHAPE
THEN ADD LASH
ADD DETAILS LAST

BREAKS IN HAIR

USE S-CURVES IN HAIR DESIGN

126

KEEP EYEBROW WITHIN FACE CONTOUR

HAIR SWEEPS OVER THIS SIDE AS HEAD TURNS

MAINTAIN HIGH CHEEKBONE

IN PROFILE, NOSE IS REPRESENTED WITH ONE LINE FOR EDGE AND ONE LINE FOR NOSTRIL

CHEST IS SAME AS HEAD VOLUME

START WITH SIMPLE SHAPES

SOFT LINE STROKES

NO? NOT RECTANGULAR

NO? TOO MATURE

MULAN IS 6-1/2 HEADS TALL

Mulan as Soldier

MULAN BECOMES A SOLDIER TO SAVE HER ELDERLY FATHER'S LIFE. SHE DEFIES TRADITION, DOING WHAT SHE BELIEVES IS RIGHT. THE FILM'S ARTISTS HAVE FOLLOWED HER DARING LEAD AND TREATED HER "SOLDIER" LOOK WITH AN UNCONVENTIONAL APPROACH. HER BASIC FEATURES ARE THE SAME, BUT SLIGHT CHANGES HAVE BEEN MADE TO HELP HIDE HER FEMININITY. HERE ARE SOME SECRETS TO DRAWING MULAN AS A SOLDIER:

ON FRONT VIEW, MULAN'S HAIR BUN LOOKS LIKE MICKEY'S EARS

WIDOW'S PEAK

HAIR IS CLOSER TO HEAD WHEN PULLED BACK

SLIGHTLY SMALLER EYES; EYE HAS NO "TAIL" LASH OR LID INDICATION LIKE "NORMAL" MULAN EYES

EARS STICK OUT PROMINENTLY

SLIGHTLY ANGLED-OUT JAWLINE

LIPS ARE SLIGHTLY LESS CURVY THAN ON "NORMAL" MULAN AND ARE NATURAL IN COLOR

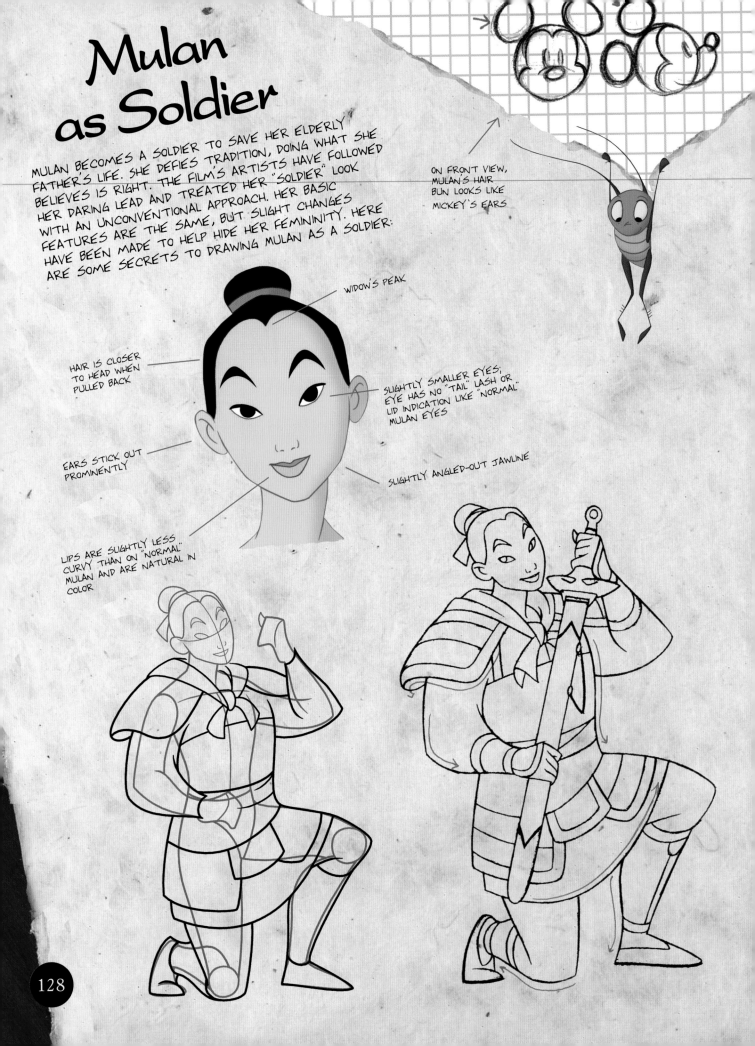

WATCH SPACE HERE

NO!

TOO WIDE

TOO SMALL

SHOW SOME THICKNESS OF HAIR

S-CURVE SHALLOW BRIDGE

EYE CLOSE TO NOSE

SLIGHT OVERBITE

EVEN WHEN SHE IS IN ARMOR, RETAIN MULAN'S GRACEFUL SHAPES

MULAN'S FATHER'S SWORD THAT SHE TAKES WITH HER TO THE ARMY

Khan

YEARS AGO, MULAN'S FATHER, FA ZHOU, RODE ON KHAN'S STURDY BACK INTO COMBAT. WHEN FA ZHOU RETURNED HOME VICTORIOUS, THE WELL-TRAINED WAR HORSE RETIRED TO A LIFE AS MULAN'S FAITHFUL FRIEND. HE'S SO CLOSE TO MULAN THAT THE HORSE EVEN MIRRORS HER EMOTIONS. YET WHEN SHE IS IN DANGER, KHAN'S BRAVERY SAVES MULAN AND HER FRIENDS FROM CERTAIN DEATH IN THE AVALANCHE. THINK OF HIS POWER AND SPEED WHILE YOU DRAW THIS MASSIVE HORSE.

EAR IS SHAPED LIKE QUILL PEN TIP

MUZZLE SHAPED LIKE A HATCHET

CURVED NECK

TAIL HAS BONE THAT CREATES SOME STIFFNESS AT TOP

THIS SIDE OF NECK IS FAIRLY STRAIGHT

TIP OF SHOULDER IS HIGHER THAN TIP OF CHEST

NOTE FLOW OF LEGS

WHEN JUST STANDING, HIS BACK LEGS ARE FAIRLY STRAIGHT

NO FOXTAILS!

USE CRISSCROSS DESIGN TO CONSTRUCT LEGS

131

Cri-Kee

THIS LITTLE CRICKET WAS GIVEN TO MULAN FOR LUCK—AND HE TAKES HIS JOB VERY SERIOUSLY. WHEN MULAN SETS OUT ON HER DANGEROUS QUEST, CRI-KEE CONVINCES MUSHU THAT THEY SHOULD GO AFTER MULAN AND ASSIST HER. HIS CAREFUL, SENSITIVE MANNER IS A COMPLETE CONTRAST TO THAT OF THE BRAZEN DRAGON, MUSHU. ALTHOUGH CRI-KEE DOESN'T SPEAK, MUSHU UNDERSTANDS HIS CHIRPS, AND THANKS TO THE EXPRESSIVE ANIMATION OF DISNEY ARTISTS, WE UNDERSTAND CRI-KEE TOO. TRY TO COPY THEIR STYLE IN BRINGING CRI-KEE TO LIFE.

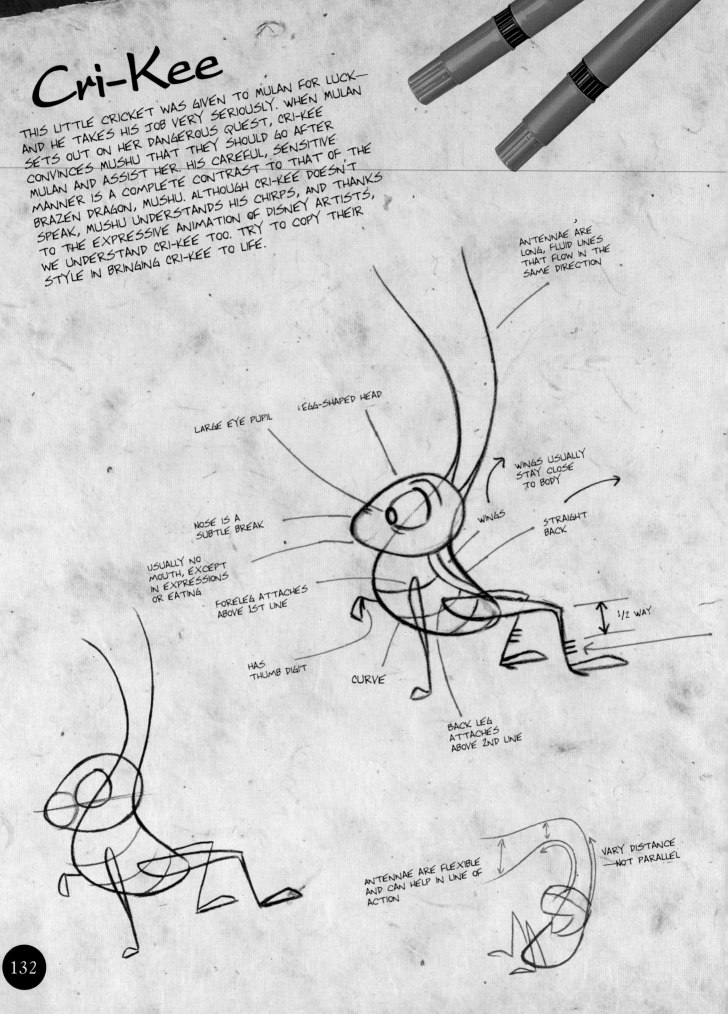

ANTENNAE ARE LONG, FLUID LINES THAT FLOW IN THE SAME DIRECTION

LARGE EYE PUPIL

EGG-SHAPED HEAD

WINGS USUALLY STAY CLOSE TO BODY

WINGS

STRAIGHT BACK

NOSE IS A SUBTLE BREAK

USUALLY NO MOUTH, EXCEPT IN EXPRESSIONS OR EATING

FORELEG ATTACHES ABOVE 1ST LINE

1/2 WAY

HAS THUMB DIGIT

CURVE

BACK LEG ATTACHES ABOVE 2ND LINE

ANTENNAE ARE FLEXIBLE AND CAN HELP IN LINE OF ACTION

VARY DISTANCE—NOT PARALLEL

NO!
NOT UPRIGHT

HEAD CONNECTS
WIDE ON BODY

3 LEG HAIRS
ARE STIFF

BODY IS ONLY
A LITTLE LARGER
THAN HEAD

Mushu

MUSHU HAS A BIG MOUTH FOR A LITTLE GUY—FIGURATIVELY SPEAKING, THAT IS. HIS BIG-SHOT TALK GOT HIM INTO TROUBLE WITH MULAN'S FAMILY ANCESTORS. NOW HE'S DETERMINED TO HELP MULAN, ALTHOUGH HE'S ONLY AS TALL AS HER KNEE. BUT YOU CAN DRAW HIM ON A LARGER SCALE TO SHOW OFF HIS CATFISH WHISKERS AND COW EARS. NOTE THAT HIS SNAKELIKE BODY FLOWS CONTINUOUSLY FROM THE TIP OF HIS TAIL TO HIS MOUTH.

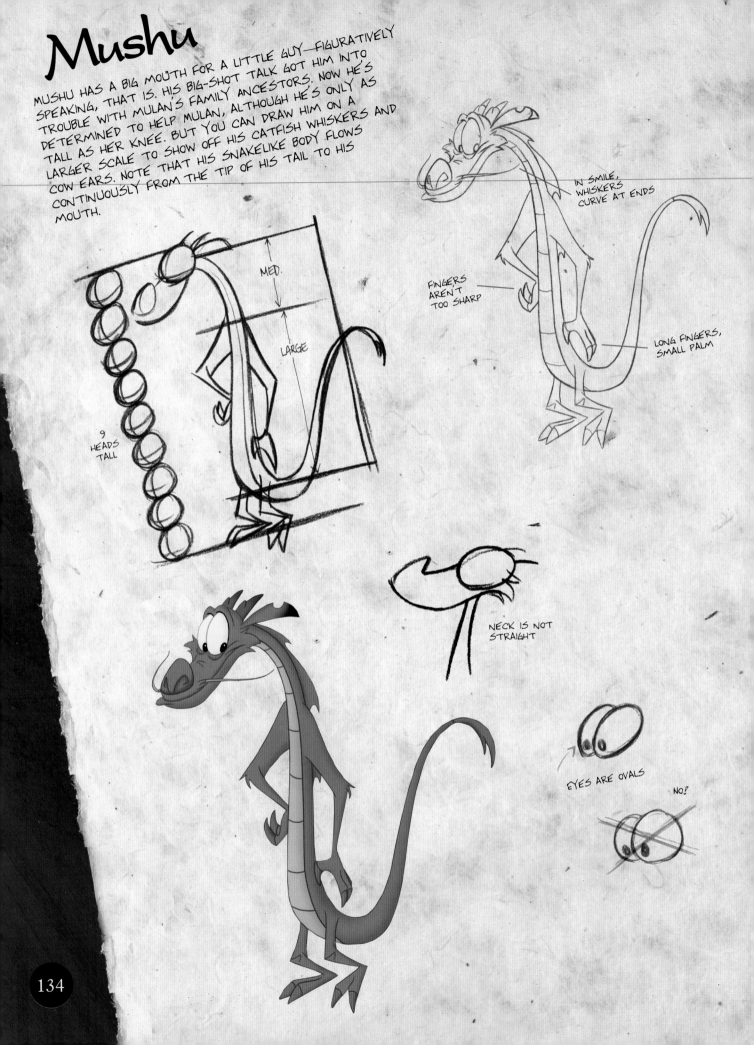

IN SMILE, WHISKERS CURVE AT ENDS

FINGERS AREN'T TOO SHARP

LONG FINGERS, SMALL PALM

MED.

LARGE

9 HEADS TALL

NECK IS NOT STRAIGHT

EYES ARE OVALS

NO?

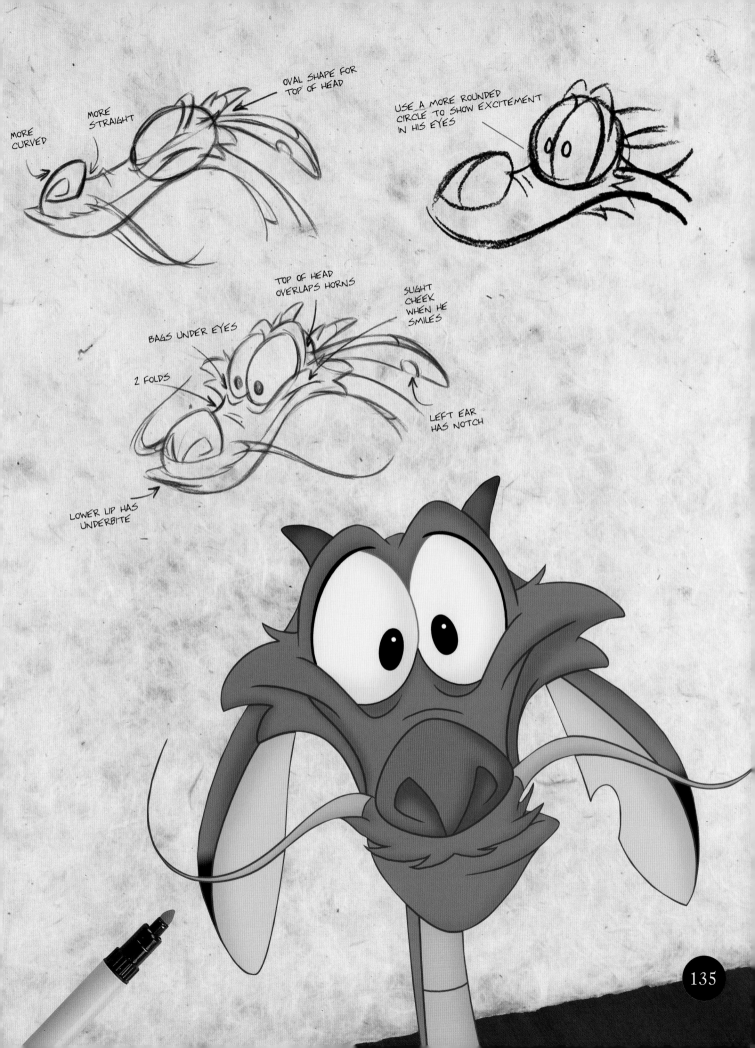

MORE
CURVED

MORE
STRAIGHT

OVAL SHAPE FOR
TOP OF HEAD

USE A MORE ROUNDED
CIRCLE TO SHOW EXCITEMENT
IN HIS EYES

TOP OF HEAD
OVERLAPS HORNS

SLIGHT
CHEEK
WHEN HE
SMILES

BAGS UNDER EYES

2 FOLDS

LEFT EAR
HAS NOTCH

LOWER LIP HAS
UNDERBITE

How to Draw
POCAHONTAS

Pocahontas

The beautiful Pocahontas has a strong, noble face with high cheekbones, piercing eyes, and flowing black hair.

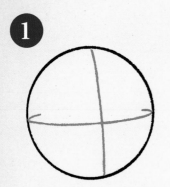

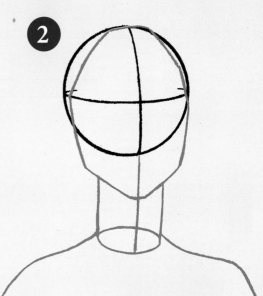

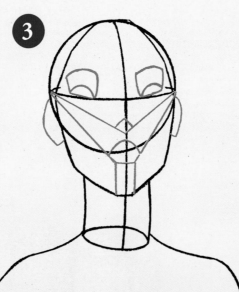

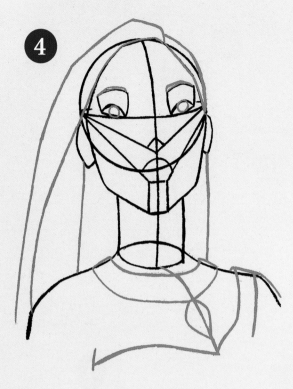

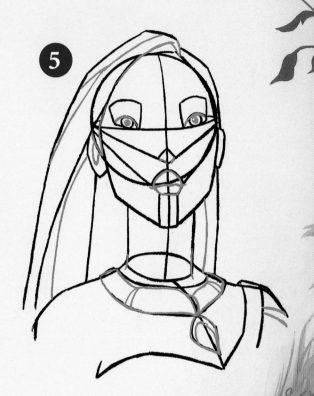

The tip of Pocahontas's nose should be very close to her upper lip.

Pocahontas

Pocahontas's body is athletic yet feminine. She stands with her shoulders back and her head held high.

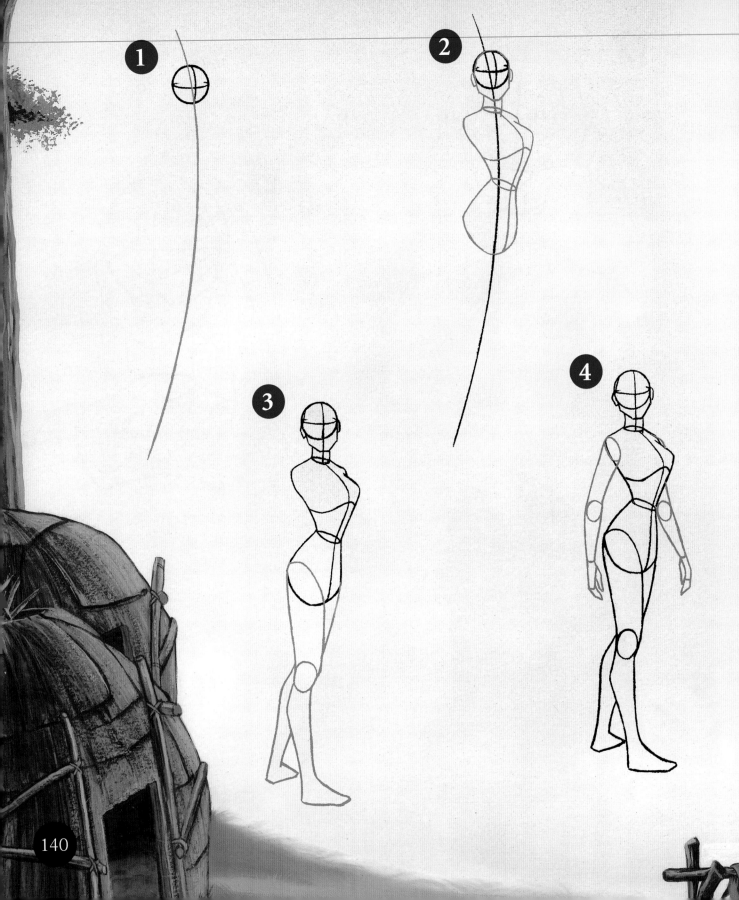

5

6

7

Meeko and Flit

Meeko and Flit are always in motion. Some of their common poses are below.